JUDGMENT
LEADERSHIP

JUDGMENT LEADERSHIP

*Decision Integrity
Under Pressure*

Dr. Hugo Velazco

The most important work is often the least visible.

Contents

For those who carried responsibility without always being seen—and for those who learned to put it down before it took more than it should.

Author's Note

This book was written for people who carry responsibility long after the meeting ends, when choices follow them home, when consequences linger, and when clarity must be maintained without certainty.

Not the kind of responsibility that comes with a title or a role description, but the quieter kind—the sense that if something fails, it will land on you. The kind that sharpens judgment for a while, then slowly narrows it. The kind that keeps work moving while something else erodes underneath.

I have spent years working alongside leaders who are competent, committed, and deeply invested in the people they serve. Many of them are not struggling because they lack skill or effort. They are struggling because the systems they operate inside reward endurance more than clarity, and speed more than containment. Over time, pressure becomes personal, even when the source is structural.

In my advisory work, I sit with leaders in moments where there is no clean resolution, only a decision that must be made and consequences that must be carried. Over time I began using a simple name for the discipline required in those environments: **Judgment Leadership**. In this book, Judgment Leadership means **decision integrity under pressure**, the capacity to decide and follow through in a way that remains coherent with responsibility, authority, and consequences when conditions compress.

The aim is not perfect decisions; it is decisions that remain intact when pressure tries to distort them.

This book is not an argument against pressure. Pressure is part of leadership. It sharpens priorities and exposes what matters. But pressure without structure quietly extracts a cost. It distorts judgment, fragments attention, and turns capable leaders into single points of failure—often without anyone noticing until something breaks.

You will not find motivation here. You will not find productivity techniques, optimization strategies, or prescriptions for doing more with less. This is also not a book about decision integrity as toughness, grit, or emotional performance. Those frames often ask leaders to adapt endlessly to conditions that remain unchanged.

Instead, this book is about containment, how work is shaped so pressure can be carried without consuming the people inside it. Containment is not comfort; it is what protects **decision integrity** when urgency rises.

The stories and patterns you will encounter come from many settings: technical environments, human systems, organizational change, and personal leadership transitions. Some details are composite by design, not to obscure truth, but to protect it. What matters here is not the industry or the role, but the behavior of work under pressure—and the ways leaders respond when responsibility accumulates faster than capacity.

You may recognize yourself in these pages. If you do, that recognition is not meant to provoke action immediately. It is meant to slow the moment just enough to see what is already happening. The most durable leadership shifts rarely begin with solutions. They begin with orientation.

This book unfolds gradually. Early chapters focus on pressure as it is experienced. Later chapters introduce structure—not as control, but as support. Reflection appears only after recognition is established. Practice is offered as experimentation, not instruction. Nothing here is designed to be rushed.

If you are reading this as part of a leadership role, a facilitation context, or a shared conversation, the book will give you language and posture. It will not give you scripts. That work happens in rooms, not on pages.

My hope is simple: that this book helps you notice where pressure is accumulating, where responsibility has become too concentrated, and where clarity—held consistently—can change how work behaves over time.

Nothing here asks you to carry more.

It asks you to hold differently.

Introduction

I. The Problem Is Not What It Looks Like

Most leadership challenges don't begin as crises. They begin as patterns that work—until they don't.

Capable people take on responsibility because it matters. They step in when something falters. They stay late, answer the message no one else responds to, and make decisions others hesitate to claim. For a while, this works. Progress continues. Problems are contained. The system appears stable.

Over time, something shifts. The work still moves, but it relies more heavily on a few individuals to hold it together. Responsibility concentrates quietly. What once felt like commitment begins to feel personal. Not because leaders are fragile or unskilled, but because the environment has learned to lean on them.

When strain finally becomes visible, it is often misnamed. Leaders are told to manage stress better, build resilience, or find balance. The assumption is that the problem lives inside the person. In many cases, it does not.

The problem is not a lack of effort.
The problem is not a lack of competence.
The problem is that pressure has nowhere to go.

When pressure has nowhere to go, it migrates into people. The first casualty is rarely performance. It is judgment.

II. Pressure Is Not the Enemy

Pressure is part of leadership. It sharpens priorities. It clarifies stakes. In the short term, it can even improve performance.

The issue is not pressure itself, but what happens when pressure is absorbed without structure. When environments reward endurance more than clarity, leaders adapt by carrying more. They make themselves useful by becoming available. They stabilize work by absorbing volatility personally.

This works—until it doesn't.

Pressure without containment distorts judgment. It shortens recovery cycles. It turns speed into a substitute for clarity and urgency into a default posture. Over time, leaders become single points of failure without ever being named as such.

What looks like strength from the outside often feels like depletion from within.

III. What Happens When Responsibility Concentrates

When responsibility concentrates, a predictable pattern emerges.

Leaders over-function. They anticipate problems before others see them. They intervene early, often silently. Wins are absorbed and forgotten. Failures linger. Memory becomes selective, shaped by what required recovery rather than what held.

The system appears resilient because it keeps moving. The cost is paid privately. Judgment narrows. Attention fragments. Rest becomes shallow. What once felt purposeful begins to feel heavy.

This is not burnout as collapse. It is erosion.

By the time something breaks, it is rarely the first failure. It is the moment when accumulated strain can no longer be carried quietly.

iv. What This Book Is — and Is Not

This book introduces **Judgment Leadership**: the discipline of maintaining **decision integrity under pressure**. It focuses on what happens when responsibility accumulates faster than clarity, and on the structural conditions that allow leaders to decide without becoming the containment layer themselves.

> This is not a productivity book.
> It is not a manual for doing more with less.
> It is not therapy, and it is not a call for
> toughness or grit.

If you remember one phrase, make it this: Judgment Leadership is decision integrity under pressure. Everything else in the book supports that claim.

You will not be asked to perform decision integrity or optimize yourself endlessly to fit environments that remain unchanged. The aim here is not to help you endure more, but to help work hold differently.

v. How the Book Unfolds

The book moves deliberately.

The early chapters stay close to lived experience—pressure as it is felt, not theorized. They establish context and credibility without instruction. Middle chapters turn inward, focusing on clarity, orientation, and the quiet disciplines that prevent strain from becoming personal. Later chapters introduce structure that allows leadership to function without reliance on heroics.

Reflection appears only after recognition. Practice is offered as experimentation, not requirement. Nothing in this book is designed to be rushed.

The order matters.

vi. How to Read This Book

This book can be read straight through, but it is designed to function as a reference. Return to it when pressure rises, when responsibility becomes concentrated, or when decision quality begins to narrow. Use it to restore orientation before you attempt solutions.

You may read it straight through.
You may read it slowly, returning to certain sections.
You may read it alongside your work, or as
    preparation for conversation.

Some readers will recognize themselves immediately. Others will recognize colleagues or systems they are part of. Both responses are valid.

The book does not ask for immediate action. It asks for attention—held long enough to notice where pressure accumulates and how responsibility is distributed.

The pages are intentionally designed with generous margins so readers may write reflections and observations alongside the text. Over time, the book can become a record of how your understanding evolves under pressure.

VII. Turning Toward Experience

This book does not begin with theory.

It begins with pressure as it is actually experienced—late at night, between decisions, in moments where leadership feels less like direction and more like carrying. The chapters that follow stay close to those moments, not to dramatize them, but to understand what they reveal.

The work begins there.

CHAPTER 1

Hidden Cracks

Judgment rarely breaks in the moment leadership becomes visible. It breaks earlier—when pressure accumulates without a place to land, and when responsibility concentrates without being named. This chapter begins there, because Judgment Leadership starts long before a crisis: at the first signs that decision integrity is narrowing.

Jose's Story

DIARY ENTRY, OCTOBER 2024

It's past midnight in my Torrance office. A text from Zara flashes the way it always does when pressure stacks without release. I don't answer right away. I tell myself I'll respond after one more email, one more task, one more thing finished.

I look at a photo of Miguel—mid-kick on the soccer field, caught in motion and sunlight. I keep it on my desk as a reminder. Not to stay motivated. Not to prove competence. But to stay present for the people who matter.

At home, Miguel is quiet tonight, surrounded by art supplies and unfinished projects. He doesn't say much. I recognize that look—the one where something is being carried without words. Some nights, I feel the cracks more than the strength.

I miss games when systems fail. Watching other fathers at the sidelines, I tell myself it's temporary. That the pressure will ease. That this is just how leadership works. Sleep comes in fragments. Even on good days, I'm already tired.

VitalTrack tells me I'm fine. The number looks optimistic. Strong, even. What it doesn't show is what's happening beneath the surface. Strain doesn't disappear just because I keep going.

Introducing Jose's workplace

Jose's organization looks stable from the outside. The metrics are strong. The team is capable. There are no visible crises demanding immediate attention.

Yet something is off.

Deadlines hold, but at a cost. Conversations are efficient, but thin. Decisions are made quickly, then quietly revisited later. Pressure accumulates—inside people and across the organization—without any single breaking point.

What feels like individual fatigue often signals something larger.

What follows is not a failure of effort, but something quieter.

The system continues to perform. It absorbs strain. It adapts. But adaptation has a price, especially when it becomes the default response to every new demand.

Where the Cracks Appear

Cracks rarely announce themselves. They don't arrive as breakdowns or visible mistakes. They appear as small accommodations made repeatedly—shortcuts justified, conversations delayed, discomfort absorbed rather than examined.

Responsibility begins to drift. Not because anyone abandons it, but because it spreads thin. People carry more than they should, longer than they can sustain.

This erosion occurs in judgment, not just performance.

At first, it looks like resilience.

Over time, it becomes something else.

Pressure Without Release

Pressure does not always demand action. Often, it waits. It accumulates in decision loops, in unspoken expectations, in the space between what is said and what is actually happening.

Systems fail internally or structurally long before they fail visibly.

What makes this dangerous is not the presence of pressure, but the absence of recognition. When strain is

normalized, it becomes invisible. When it becomes invisible, it stops being addressed.

What Remains Unsaid

Jose doesn't describe himself as overwhelmed. He wouldn't use that word. He would say he's managing. That things are under control. That this is what leadership requires.

He isn't wrong.

And yet, something is already shifting.

What matters here is not resolution, but recognition.

The cost is not immediate collapse. It is quiet misalignment—between responsibility and capacity, between effort and judgment, between what is carried and what is acknowledged.

Holding the Tension

This book does not rush to resolve these moments. It returns to them, slowly.

Because the most consequential failures in leadership rarely come from what breaks suddenly. They come from what holds too long without being named.

Through My Eyes

Following José through these moments, what stands out isn't the technology or the metrics—it's how pressure accumulates when responsibility has nowhere to land. Under sustained strain, work often becomes refuge. Over time, that refuge turns into overextension. Health symptoms surface quietly. Judgment narrows. Confidence erodes without announcing itself.

I've seen this pattern repeatedly in high-performing leaders. When relational stress intensifies, leaders compensate by carrying more, not less. The system may hold for a while. The person absorbs the cost. By the time cracks appear, they are often mistaken for individual weakness rather than a signal of systemic overload.

What I've seen repeatedly is that capable leaders begin compensating for unclear structure by carrying more personally. Over time, judgment narrows and decisions become reactive, not because leaders lack skill, but because pressure outruns clarity. The disciplines in this book are designed to protect **decision integrity under pressure:** noticing strain earlier, clarifying what matters, and interrupting escalation before it compounds.

José's experience reflects this dynamic. From the outside, progress is visible. Inside, self-doubt grows louder just as responsibility expands. The contradiction is familiar: leaders helping build systems designed to support others while quietly absorbing strain themselves.

What matters is not avoiding pressure altogether—that's unrealistic—but learning how to recognize it, respond to it, and recover without losing oneself in the process. This is where decision integrity becomes real: not as performance, but as capacity sustained over time.

Jose's Diary Entry
(CONTINUED)

The promise I made to Miguel—to be more present—kept surfacing as work pressed in. Around the same time, Sarah asked for a meeting. She leads our Global UX Platform, and even through the screen, her exhaustion was visible. Uptime had improved. Sprint velocity was up. The system was performing. She wasn't.

We talked through the numbers with the team. Heads nodded, but the confidence felt rehearsed. Sustaining this pace didn't feel certain. That was when I remembered a recent advisory conversation—being asked to slow down long enough to see what was actually happening, not just what was working. I decided to apply that discipline with the team.

We began with small check-ins. Nothing elaborate. Just enough space to catch friction early. Sarah named her self-doubt without dramatizing it. Others followed. The shift was quiet, but real. The work didn't stop. It steadied.

Later that week, I sat alone at Fifth Street Café and organized what I was carrying into three simple columns—what was holding, what was threatening, and what required action.

What's holding

- Slowly rebuilding my bond with Miguel
- Team morale, still intact despite the strain

What's threatening

- Victor's unresolved claims, delaying a major client decision
- Ongoing conflict with Zara, bleeding into family life

What requires action

- Stay consistent with Miguel, even when work crowds the edges
- Continue using structured reflection to stabilize decision integrity under pressure

This wasn't new. It was familiar. And it worked before. Structured reflection gave me a place to unload what I could not carry alone and helped the team move through conflict without fragmenting. The work regained rhythm—not because pressure disappeared, but because decisions began traveling with clearer reasoning and ownership.

I'm learning that personal strain and organizational tension often mirror each other. What's left unaddressed in one place tends to surface somewhere else. Seeing that clearly doesn't solve everything—but it keeps the damage from spreading.

Sarah's Story
TEAM MEETING TRANSCRIPT (OCTOBER 2024)

The comment arrived without warning. Victor called the interface *amateurish*. Six weeks from launch, with a partnership on the line, the word landed harder than it should have. The platform metrics told a different story—uptime had improved, sprint velocity was up—but the room went quiet. Everyone felt the risk before anyone named it.

Marcus's departure still hovered in the background. He had been the one who stabilized the APIs, the one who absorbed daily friction without asking for attention. When he left for another company, the loss felt personal. Not because the work stopped—but because the margin for error narrowed.

Priya spoke first. "The localization flow is broken. I can take it." Her confidence wasn't loud. It came from having lived inside the problem. For her, localization wasn't translation. It was making software feel native—language, rhythm, cues, behavior—so users didn't have to work to belong.

Mateo followed. "Infrastructure can hold, but only if we slow the release just enough." The suggestion wasn't popular. It was necessary.

"We're going to protect decision integrity," she said. "Priya leads the fix. Mateo keeps us stable. We move fast, but we don't let speed replace judgment."

Later, alone at her desk, the adrenaline faded. She scheduled another advisory conversation before the strain could spill further. The decision felt small. It wasn't.

Containment Without Heroics

After the decision, the work changed texture. Not faster—clearer. Testing tightened. Defects surfaced earlier instead of leaking downstream. Conversations slowed just enough to prevent rework. The system held under pressure without asking for heroics.

Victor's claims didn't disappear, but their power faded. With steadier processes in place, the noise had less room to spread. Sarah resisted the urge to respond publicly. She focused on discipline—small reviews, earlier signals, fewer assumptions. What could have unraveled became contained.

The shift showed up quietly. Incident response became coordinated. Escalations tapered. Ownership clarified. The work felt more dependable, not because risk vanished, but because it was seen sooner. Judgment returned before urgency took over.

The strain remained personal. Migraines flared. Sleep came unevenly. Still, Sarah chose continuity over collapse—documenting small, real wins and letting progress accumulate without forcing it. The pressure didn't disappear. She learned to carry it without distortion.

By the time the quarter closed, the recovery didn't look dramatic. It looked stable. And that was enough.

Before Anything Breaks

Pressure rarely announces itself as a crisis. More often, it accumulates quietly—through unresolved strain, narrowed judgment, and the steady habit of carrying what should be shared. Leadership doesn't fail in these moments because people stop caring. It falters when systems demand endurance without offering structure in return.

What holds is not intensity, speed, or resolve. What holds is containment—decisions made early, signals noticed sooner, and work shaped to support the people inside it. Decision integrity begins there, long before anything breaks.

CHAPTER 2

Facing the Fire

José's Journey

In the quiet that settles after long days, the spirals return. Pressure doesn't arrive as panic—it shows up as persistence. The quarter's demands, Victor's unresolved disruption, the constant sense of being behind even when the work moves forward. What steadies me now isn't reassurance. It's discipline.

Under pressure, leadership becomes less about having answers and more about protecting the conditions that make good decisions possible.

Through my work with leaders, I've learned to slow the moment long enough to separate what I can influence from what I can't. Not to disengage, but to regain judgment. The work continues, builds, releases, reviews, but I'm no longer trying to outrun it. I'm choosing how to meet it.

Miguel interrupts my thoughts from the hallway. "Dad... are you doing okay at work?"

The question pulls me back to a memory—sitting on the floor years ago, lining up dominoes with him, planning each move carefully before the first piece fell. That patience had quieted my breathing then. It still does. Even now, I feel my jaw loosen slightly. A reminder: response matters more than speed.

These moments anchor me. They mirror what the team needs under pressure—attention without urgency, steadiness without spectacle. Leadership, I'm learning, is less about pushing through resistance and more about creating conditions where the next move is clear.

When Pressure Redistributes

The work gives evidence. Elena's recovery effort stabilized a system others had written off. Uptime reached its target by the fourth quarter. Incident response shortened. Escalations slowed. The numbers mattered—but not for the reasons leadership decks usually claim. They mattered because they reduced noise and gave people room to think.

Still, doubt persisted. Victor's claims hadn't disappeared, and trust doesn't rebound on schedule. Progress unfolded alongside skepticism, not after it. I carried a quiet fear that the team's steadiness depended too heavily on my presence— that if I faltered, the system would follow.

At home, the contrast was sharper. Miguel's questions were simple. "Did you fix it?" he asked one night, meaning a bug he'd overheard me mention. I told him yes, then corrected myself. "We're fixing it." The distinction felt small. It wasn't.

That shift—away from singular responsibility—began to change how I showed up at work. I stopped translating every decision into certainty. I asked clearer questions. I let silence do some of the work. The team filled the space.

Pressure didn't lift. But it redistributed. And for the first time in months, the system felt less fragile because it wasn't being held by one person alone.

When Signals Surface Early

The shift became visible during an ordinary meeting. No incident. No deadline crisis. Just a review that could have drifted into autopilot.

Instead of leading with answers, I opened with a pause. The room stayed quiet longer than usual. Then someone named a concern that would normally surface weeks later. Another added a constraint we'd been working around without acknowledging. The conversation moved slower— and went further.

Sarah didn't carry the room. She shaped it. Questions replaced explanations. Assumptions were surfaced early, before they hardened into friction. What might have become another late-stage scramble stayed contained because the signals appeared sooner.

Afterward, the work felt lighter without being easier. Decisions traveled shorter distances. Ownership clarified. The system didn't rely on urgency to move forward—it relied on visibility.

This is what changed: pressure no longer demanded immediate resolution. It asked for attention. And attention, when shared, proved more durable than control.

When Tension Doesn't Escalate

The steadiness carried into moments that usually expose fault lines. During a late afternoon review, a sharp comment landed harder than intended. No one reacted immediately. The pause held. Instead of spiraling into defensiveness, the group named what had been triggered and stayed with it long enough to understand why.

What followed wasn't agreement. It was orientation. A recent win was recalled—not to soften the tension, but to restore proportion. The work hadn't been flawless, but it had been collective. That mattered. The moment passed without residue.

Later, priorities were narrowed deliberately. One objective took precedence: keeping the system stable through the next release. Tasks were reduced, ownership clarified, and check-ins shortened. Progress was reviewed not to assign blame, but to stay aligned as conditions shifted.

The pace didn't accelerate. It steadied. Fewer issues surfaced late because more were seen early. What once required correction now required attention. The difference was subtle—and decisive.

When Leadership Stops Performing

Sarah didn't announce a shift. She made it visible through consistency. In meetings, she asked fewer questions—but better ones. She stopped translating uncertainty into reassurance and let the work speak earlier. When something felt off, she named it without attaching urgency or blame.

The effect wasn't dramatic. It was stabilizing. Teams prepared sooner. Hand-offs tightened. Decisions happened before pressure narrowed the field. People stopped waiting for escalation to take something seriously.

Under the same constraints, Sarah's posture changed the room. Not by absorbing tension, but by holding it long enough for others to engage. The work didn't depend on her stamina. It depended on shared attention.

This was leadership without spectacle. And it held.

From Effort to Structure

Pressure doesn't disappear when systems improve. It changes shape. When leadership stops absorbing strain and starts shaping conditions, work becomes more honest—and more durable. Signals surface sooner. Decisions travel shorter distances. Responsibility redistributes without loss of momentum.

This is how decision integrity moves from effort to structure. Not through force, but through clarity sustained long enough to hold.

INTERLUDE:
The Cost of Carrying Everything

Pressure rarely breaks people all at once. It accumulates through small, repeated moments of over-responsibility—decisions made alone, signals ignored until they harden, effort substituted for structure. Over time, carrying everything becomes a quiet identity: dependable, capable, necessary.

What often goes unnoticed is the cost. Judgment narrows. Recovery shortens. The system appears functional while decision integrity erodes underneath. Leaders mistake endurance for strength and consistency for health.

This is the moment before a different question becomes possible. Not *How do I keep going?* but *What am I holding that should no longer be carried alone?* The answer doesn't arrive through intensity. It emerges through attention—slowed just enough to notice where strain is accumulating and why.

CHAPTER 3

Debugging the Self

Jose's Story

JOURNAL LETTER TO MIGUEL, OCTOBER

Dear Miguel,

It's just after 2 a.m. in my Torrance apartment. The house is quiet except for the soft hum of my laptop. VitalTrack logs blur across the screen, but it isn't the work that has my hands shaking. It's the thought that I'm not sure whether I'm leading—or just surviving.

In these quiet hours, doubt speaks more freely. I catch myself wondering if your mom was right about me. Then I think about the way you fight back after falling behind in a game, how you keep playing even when the score isn't kind. Leadership feels like debugging live systems—every fix revealing

new vulnerabilities, every correction strengthening the whole if it's done with care.

Some nights I worry I'm failing you the way my father failed me. He was often elsewhere—choosing alcohol and distraction over presence. I don't drink the way he did, but I see how work can pull me away just as effectively. The difference, I hope, is that I'm learning to notice it sooner.

Over time, I've learned to name something I avoided for years: sustainable leadership isn't about hiding weakness or pushing through it. It's about building systems—at work and at home—that don't require someone to break for them to function. I'm trying to learn that lesson with you in mind, even when I don't get it right.

This work isn't just about results. It's about becoming someone you can rely on—not because I carry everything, but because I know when not to.

Love,
Dad

Sarah's Story

The question surfaced in a team meeting without accusation. "Can we keep this pace without wearing people down?" No one rushed to answer. The silence that followed was different from earlier months—less defensive, more honest.

The timing mattered. We had just completed a migration that reduced friction across the system. Workloads felt lighter. Reviews were steadier. For the first time in a while, progress didn't require constant correction. The change wasn't dramatic. It was sustainable.

What made the difference wasn't the migration itself. It was what we did next. We paused long enough to name what had worked and why. Wins were captured without celebration. Breakdowns were discussed without blame. The reflection wasn't retrospective theater—it was orientation.

That discipline carried into the next sprint. A gap in our analytics surfaced early, flagged by a teammate who would previously have waited. We adjusted before it cascaded. Nothing heroic happened. The system simply held.

I'm beginning to understand that progress isn't secured by momentum alone. It's secured by attention—applied consistently, before strain forces the issue.

Sarah begins documenting

What Sarah discovered wasn't insight. It was pattern.

Once the work was written down—wins captured without commentary, breakdowns logged without self-critique—something shifted. The noise thinned. What remained was usable. Decisions no longer felt reactive because the context was visible. She didn't feel calmer. She felt oriented.

The act of documenting changed how strain registered in her body. Pressure still arrived, but it no longer demanded immediate resolution. It waited. That alone altered her judgment. What once felt personal revealed itself as systemic. What once felt urgent became specific.

Over time, the record told a quieter story than memory ever could. Progress showed up in small intervals. Setbacks lost their power to define the whole. The work didn't ask her to be resilient. It asked her to be precise.

This is where recovery began—not with relief, but with clarity sustained long enough to trust.

Letter to Sophie and Noah OCTOBER 2024

What became clear was this: reflection works only when it is contained.

When Sarah began documenting consistently—not to explain herself, not to justify outcomes—the record stopped feeling like evidence and started functioning as orientation. This is decision integrity in practice: a record strong enough to prevent pressure from rewriting reality. The entries were brief. Factual. Unemotional. And because of that, they could be trusted.

Patterns emerged without force. A recurring delay tied to the same handoff. A rise in tension before certain reviews. Small wins that never registered emotionally, but mattered operationally. None of it required interpretation at first. Seeing it was enough.

This is where reflection shifted from inward to useful. Not as rumination, but as signal. The work didn't ask for insight on demand. It offered it gradually, once attention stayed long enough to notice.

Capacity returned this way—not as relief, but as margin. Decisions felt less loaded. Corrections felt less personal. The system gained room to adjust without consuming the people inside it.

This was not improvement through effort.
It was clarity through containment.

Composite Case

A senior leader described feeling calm only when everyone else was overwhelmed. When systems were stable, she felt unnecessary. Chaos gave her relevance. It took time to recognize that what felt like competence was actually over-functioning.

Another leader kept detailed notes, but only after failures. Wins passed undocumented. Over months, the record told a distorted story—one of constant recovery without progress. The work appeared fragile because the lens was incomplete.

A third leader avoided writing anything down at all. Reflection felt indulgent, even risky. Without a record, every setback felt new. Each decision carried the weight of the last unresolved moment.

None of these leaders lacked skill or commitment. What they lacked was containment. Once attention was structured—captured consistently, without judgment—the same environments felt manageable. Pressure didn't disappear. It became legible.

REFLECTION

1. Where have you been relying on memory instead of record—and what might that be costing you?

2. What signals do you notice only after pressure accumulates?

3. Which responsibilities feel personal, even though they may be structural?

PRACTICE

1. For one week, capture a brief daily record of work: one thing that held, one thing that strained, one thing that clarified. No interpretation.

2. In your next meeting, pause before responding and note what surfaces without urgency.

When Clarity Holds

Clarity doesn't arrive through force. It arrives when attention is structured long enough to notice what experience is already offering. When reflection is contained, it stops circling and starts orienting.

This is how capacity returns—not as relief, but as margin. The work holds because it no longer requires constant interpretation. What once felt personal becomes legible. What once demanded endurance begins to support judgment instead.

CHAPTER 4

Containment

When Pressure Has Somewhere to Land

Containment is often mistaken for control. In practice, it has little to do with authority or oversight. It has everything to do with whether pressure has somewhere to land without being absorbed by a single person.

In environments without containment, leaders become the structure by default. They remember what others forget. They carry context across meetings. They absorb volatility so the work can continue uninterrupted. The system appears functional because someone is holding it together.

Containment changes that dynamic. It does not eliminate pressure; it distributes it. Decisions are documented. Ownership is explicit. Signals surface early enough to be addressed without urgency. The work itself begins to hold what individuals no longer need to carry alone.

This shift is subtle. It rarely announces itself as improvement. More often, it shows up as steadiness. Fewer late-stage

corrections. Fewer personal interventions. Fewer moments where leadership requires heroics to prevent collapse.

Containment is not about doing less. It is about making pressure legible, so judgment can remain intact when conditions tighten.

When Leaders Stop Absorbing the System

José noticed the change first in what he no longer had to remember.

Details that once lived in his head—handoffs, exceptions, unresolved decisions—were now visible to others. Not because the work had become simpler, but because it had become shareable. Context moved with the work instead of staying trapped with him.

At first, the shift felt uncomfortable. He caught himself scanning for what might fall through, ready to intervene.

When nothing did, the instinct lingered anyway. Years of absorbing the system don't disappear just because conditions improve.

What surprised him most was not relief, but judgment. Meetings felt different. Decisions landed with less weight because they no longer carried hidden dependencies. When pressure arrived, it did not collapse inward. It spread across clear ownership and documented context.

José realized that much of what he had called leadership was actually compensation. He had been holding the system together so it could avoid learning how to hold itself. Once containment was present, his role changed—not to disengage, but to see more clearly where leadership actually mattered.

This was not a loss of control.

It was the return of proportion.

When Work Holds What People Shouldn't

The difference is easiest to see in moments of strain.

Without containment, pressure moves upward. Ambiguity follows the same path. Leaders become the place where unresolved work accumulates—questions, exceptions, partial decisions. The system stays in motion because someone is carrying what it cannot hold on its own.

With containment, the movement changes. Pressure is distributed across visible ownership. Decisions travel with context. Gaps surface early enough to be addressed without escalation. The work itself absorbs variation instead of passing it silently to the top.

This is not about removing accountability. It is about relocating it. When accountability lives in people rather than in structure, leadership becomes endurance. When accountability lives in the work, leadership becomes judgment.

The cost of the first approach is familiar: late corrections, fragile progress, and leaders who feel indispensable long after they should not have to be. The benefit of the second is quieter. Fewer emergencies. Clearer tradeoffs. A system that adjusts without requiring someone to hold everything together.

Containment does not reduce responsibility.
It changes where responsibility lives.

What Containment Is Not

Containment is often misunderstood because it is quiet.

It is not control. Control tightens oversight when trust erodes. Containment does the opposite—it makes trust unnecessary by making the work visible enough to stand on its own.

It is not disengagement. Leaders do not step back because they care less. They step back because the system no longer requires constant intervention to function.

It is not bureaucracy. Containment does not add layers for the sake of order. When structure becomes heavy, it signals that clarity is missing, not that more process is needed.

It is also not emotional detachment. Leaders still care deeply. What changes is where care is expressed. Instead of absorbing strain personally, leaders shape conditions so strain can be carried without becoming personal.

Containment fails when it is treated as a tool. It works only when it is held as a discipline—applied consistently, without urgency, and adjusted as the work changes.

A Composite Case: Containment in Practice

In a regional healthcare organization, escalation had become routine. Small issues moved quickly to senior leaders, not because staff lacked capability, but because no one was certain where responsibility ended. Decisions were revisited repeatedly. Context lived in conversations rather than in the work itself.

The turning point did not come from new policies or tools. It came from a change in posture. Leaders began insisting—quietly—that decisions travel with documented rationale and clear ownership. Not exhaustive detail. Just enough to be shared.

At first, the change felt slower. Questions lingered longer at the edges instead of being resolved immediately. Some leaders worried this meant disengagement. What they began to notice instead was learning. Teams adjusted without escalation. Errors surfaced earlier, when correction was still light.

Over time, senior leaders were pulled in less often, but more intentionally. Their attention shifted from triage to judgment. When pressure rose, it spread across the system instead of collapsing into a few individuals.

The organization did not become calmer overnight. It became steadier. And in that steadiness, leaders regained capacity without having to perform it.

REFLECTION

1. Where does pressure currently land in your work—and who absorbs it when structure is unclear?

2. What responsibilities have become personal that may actually be structural?

3. Where do you notice yourself intervening out of habit rather than necessity?

PRACTICE

1. For one week, notice where decisions escalate by default. Ask what would need to be visible or clarified for them to hold where they originate.

2. In one recurring meeting, shift from solving to documenting: what was decided, by whom, and why. Leave interpretation out.

When Structure Carries the Weight

Containment does not make work easier. It makes work honest.

When pressure has somewhere to land, leaders no longer need to absorb what the system cannot hold. Responsibility becomes visible. Decisions regain proportion. Judgment replaces endurance as the primary demand of leadership.

This shift is rarely dramatic. It does not announce itself as transformation. More often, it shows up in what no longer happens—fewer escalations, fewer late corrections, fewer moments where leadership is required to compensate for missing structure.

Containment is not the absence of strain. It is the presence of support where strain would otherwise concentrate. When work holds what people should not, leadership stops performing and begins to endure in a different way.

What follows is not about carrying more.
It is about making room.

CHAPTER 5

Capacity

When Capacity Is Misread as Endurance

Capacity is often described as energy—how much someone can take, how long they can last, how reliably they can push through. In practice, this definition confuses endurance with judgment and persistence with sustainability.

Endurance allows work to continue under strain. Capacity determines whether it should. Judgment Leadership favors capacity over endurance, because endurance can sustain motion while decision integrity quietly erodes.

When leaders are praised primarily for staying available, responding quickly, or absorbing disruption without visible impact, capacity begins to erode quietly. Decisions narrow. Recovery shortens. What looks like decision integrity from the outside becomes fragility within the system.

True capacity is not measured by output alone. It shows up in timing, proportion, and restraint. Leaders with capacity know when to act and when to wait. They can distinguish between urgency and importance because their attention is not already depleted.

Without containment, capacity is consumed compensating for missing structure. With containment, capacity becomes available for judgment. The difference is subtle but decisive. One sustains motion. The other sustains leadership.

This chapter is not about restoring energy. It is about reclaiming margin—so decisions can be made without being rushed by depletion.

When Capacity Quietly Shrinks

Capacity rarely collapses all at once. More often, it thins.

Leaders notice it first in timing. Decisions that once felt straightforward begin to feel heavier. Follow-ups multiply. Recovery from routine strain takes longer than expected. None of this signals failure. It signals load carried too long without relief.

What makes this difficult to see is that performance often remains high. Output continues. Availability is praised. From the outside, nothing appears wrong. Internally, attention narrows. Leaders rely more on habit than judgment because judgment requires margin.

This is where endurance becomes deceptive. It allows work to continue while masking the cost. The system benefits in the short term. The leader absorbs the difference.

Capacity shrinks not because leaders stop caring, but because caring without containment consumes what margin remains. When that margin disappears, everything begins to feel urgent—even when it is not.

Recognizing this early is not weakness. It is orientation. Capacity does not ask to be replenished after collapse. It asks to be protected before judgment is compromised.

When Judgment Becomes the First Casualty

José didn't experience the loss of capacity as exhaustion. He experienced it as compression.

Decisions began arriving already weighted. Tradeoffs felt tighter, even when the stakes hadn't changed. He noticed himself defaulting to familiar solutions—not because they were better, but because they required less deliberation. The work moved forward, but it did so on thinner margins.

What stood out most was how little time there was between noticing a problem and acting on it. Reflection collapsed into reaction. Not out of panic, but out of habit. There was simply no space left to hold uncertainty long enough for judgment to form.

This was not a failure of discipline. It was a predictable outcome of capacity spent compensating for strain elsewhere. The system had learned that José would absorb what it could not resolve. Over time, that absorption replaced shared judgment with personal endurance.

When containment improved, capacity did not return as energy. It returned as choice. He could pause without falling

behind. He could ask one more question before deciding. The work slowed just enough for proportion to reappear.

Capacity, he realized, is not what allows leaders to act quickly. It is what allows them to decide well when speed is no longer the point.

What Capacity Is Not

Capacity is often misunderstood because it is easiest to notice when it is gone.

It is not stamina. Stamina measures how long someone can persist under strain. Capacity determines whether persistence is still wise. Endurance without judgment may keep work moving, but it rarely keeps it sound.

It is not availability. Being reachable at all times creates the appearance of responsiveness while quietly eroding discernment. When every interruption is treated as urgent, nothing is held long enough to be considered fully.

It is not emotional regulation. Staying composed under pressure can mask the absence of margin. Calm becomes performance when leaders are required to manage themselves instead of shaping the conditions around them.

It is also not recovery alone. Rest restores energy, but it does not rebuild capacity if the work continues to demand constant compensation. Without changes in structure, recovery becomes a brief pause between drains.

Capacity is not a personal trait to be cultivated in isolation. It is a property of how work is arranged. When systems rely on individual endurance, capacity will always be temporary.

A Composite Case: Capacity Under Load

In a large public agency, leadership turnover had slowed decision-making without reducing workload. Interim roles multiplied. Approvals stacked. Senior leaders stayed available to prevent delays, stepping in wherever friction appeared.

From the outside, the system looked resilient. Deadlines were met. Crises were contained. Internally, judgment thinned. Decisions defaulted to precedent. Novel problems were treated as exceptions to be managed rather than signals to be examined.

What changed was not effort, but arrangement. Leaders began limiting where escalation was permitted and clarifying which decisions required deliberation rather than speed. Not all issues moved faster. Some moved more slowly by design.

Over time, capacity returned in unexpected ways. Meetings shortened because fewer issues arrived pre-escalated. Leaders noticed they could hold uncertainty longer without feeling behind. The system absorbed fluctuation without immediately transferring it upward.

The work did not become lighter.
It became more proportionate.

REFLECTION

1. Where in your work has endurance been mistaken for capacity?

2. What decisions currently feel heavier than their actual stakes—and what might that suggest about margin?

3. Where has speed quietly replaced judgment in ways that now feel difficult to reverse?

PRACTICE

1. For one week, notice which decisions you rush not because they are urgent, but because holding them feels costly. Name what makes them feel that way.

2. Identify one recurring escalation and ask what would need to change structurally for judgment to return without delay.

When Judgment Has Room

Capacity does not disappear because leaders stop caring. It disappears because caring becomes the only mechanism holding the work together.

When endurance substitutes for structure, judgment quietly thins. Decisions compress. Timing narrows. What once felt deliberate begins to feel reactive—not because the stakes have changed, but because margin has.

Rest alone cannot restore capacity when the work continues to demand compensation. Capacity returns when leaders are no longer required to absorb what the system has not learned to hold. When containment is present, judgment regains space. Choices regain proportion. Leadership no longer depends on how much strain someone can tolerate.

Capacity is not the ability to carry more.
It is the ability to decide without
being rushed by depletion.

José noticed the cost of endurance most clearly in the evenings—where decisions were faster, but presence was shorter.

CHAPTER 6

Alignment

When Alignment Is Assumed

Alignment is often treated as agreement. When people nod, when plans move forward, when conflict stays quiet, alignment is presumed to exist. In practice, those signals are unreliable.

Teams can agree and still pull in different directions. They can execute efficiently while optimizing for incompatible priorities. Misalignment rarely announces itself as resistance. More often, it shows up as friction—work that moves, but strains; progress that requires constant coordination to sustain.

What makes alignment difficult is that it is usually inferred rather than named. Goals are implied. Tradeoffs are left unspoken. Leaders assume shared understanding because the cost of slowing down feels higher than the risk of drift.

Under pressure, this assumption becomes expensive. Decisions multiply. Context fragments. People work harder to compensate for unclear priorities, mistaking effort for cohesion. The system appears busy, even productive, while pulling itself apart quietly.

Alignment is not a feeling and it is not consensus. Alignment protects decision integrity by making tradeoffs explicit before pressure forces them implicitly. It is the ongoing discipline of making priorities visible enough that work can coordinate without constant intervention. When alignment is assumed rather than established, leadership becomes translation—repeating, clarifying, correcting— work the system should be able to do on its own.

When Priorities Compete Quietly

Misalignment rarely looks like disagreement. It looks like parallel effort.

Teams move quickly on what feels urgent to them. Decisions are made locally, with good intent. Each action makes sense in isolation. Over time, the work begins to compete with itself. Dependencies multiply. Corrections arrive late, when reversing course is costly.

What's missing is not communication, but hierarchy of importance. When priorities are not made explicit, people fill the gap with their own judgment. That judgment is shaped by role, proximity to risk, and recent pressure. Alignment erodes not because people disagree, but because they are optimizing for different signals.

Leaders often respond by clarifying again—restating goals, repeating direction, adding updates. This helps temporarily. It does not resolve the underlying problem. Alignment does not fail because messages were unclear. It fails because tradeoffs were never named.

When priorities are visible, coordination becomes easier. People know what to defer, what to escalate, and what to let go. Work moves with fewer collisions, not because effort increases, but because direction stabilizes.

Alignment is not the absence of conflict.
It is the presence of shared reference points
    that allow conflict to be resolved without
    constant translation.

When Leaders Become Translators

Sarah noticed the shift in her calendar before she named it anywhere else. More time was spent reconciling decisions than making them. Meetings multiplied, not to resolve conflict, but to explain why parallel work had collided.

None of the teams were off course. Each was responding to real pressure. What was missing was a shared sense of what mattered *most* when not everything could move forward at once. In the absence of that clarity, Sarah became the bridge—context carrier, priority interpreter, decision harmonizer.

At first, this felt like leadership. She was helping. Progress resumed. But the pattern persisted. The same questions returned in different forms. Each clarification solved a moment without stabilizing the system.

What she began to see was that alignment had been outsourced upward. Teams waited for translation instead of orienting themselves. The work moved, but only when she was present to connect it.

When priorities were finally named—explicitly, and with their tradeoffs intact—the need for translation decreased. Decisions held longer. Fewer explanations were required. Sarah's role shifted from continuous interpretation to occasional judgment.

Alignment didn't eliminate tension.
It reduced dependence.

What Alignment Is Not

Alignment is often confused with agreement.

When people move forward without objection, leaders assume priorities are shared. In reality, silence frequently signals uncertainty, not cohesion. Alignment that depends on consensus tends to dissolve the moment conditions change.

Alignment is also not constant communication. More updates do not resolve competing priorities. Repetition can create the appearance of clarity while leaving tradeoffs untouched. When everything is said repeatedly, nothing is decided explicitly.

It is not harmony. Healthy alignment can feel tense, especially when constraints are real. Naming what will not be pursued creates discomfort, but that discomfort is preferable to drift masked as cooperation.

Alignment is not achieved through charisma or persuasion. It does not require leaders to convince others to care

more. It requires leaders to make priorities visible enough that care can be directed without interpretation.

When alignment is treated as a feeling to be maintained, leaders spend their time managing reactions. When it is treated as a discipline, leaders shape conditions so work can coordinate without constant mediation.

A COMPOSITE CASE:
Alignment Under Constraint

In a mid-sized manufacturing firm, teams prided themselves on execution. Orders moved. Schedules held. When disruptions occurred, managers adjusted locally to keep their lanes clear. From the outside, the operation looked coordinated.

Problems emerged at the seams. Inventory was optimized for speed while quality teams slowed releases to reduce risk.

Sales commitments outpaced production capacity. Each decision made sense within its boundary. Together, they created friction that surfaced late—when rework was expensive and relationships were strained.

Leadership responded with more communication. Updates increased. Alignment meetings multiplied. What didn't change was the absence of explicit tradeoffs. No one named which priority would give way when constraints tightened.

The shift came when leaders stopped asking teams to coordinate better and began naming priorities clearly—along with what would not be optimized. Speed was preserved in some areas, deliberately sacrificed in others. Decisions held longer because the criteria for tradeoffs were visible.

Alignment did not eliminate tension. It reduced collision. Teams adjusted earlier, not because they agreed more, but because they shared reference points strong enough to guide action without translation.

REFLECTION

- Where in your work do priorities feel understood but rarely named?

- When tension arises, what decisions are being revisited instead of clarified?

- Where have you become a translator—and what does that suggest about alignment upstream?

PRACTICE

- Identify one decision that keeps resurfacing.
  Ask what tradeoff has not been made explicit.

- In an upcoming conversation, state one priority
  and one deliberate deprioritization. Notice what
  becomes easier once both are named.

When Direction Holds

Alignment is not sustained by agreement or effort. It is
sustained by clarity that holds when pressure shifts.

When priorities are assumed, leaders become translators.
They reconcile decisions after the fact, absorb friction at the
seams, and carry context the work should already contain.
Alignment appears intact only as long as someone is present
to keep it that way.

When priorities are named—along with their tradeoffs—the work begins to coordinate itself. Tension does not
disappear, but it becomes productive. Decisions travel with
reference points instead of explanations. Leadership moves
from constant mediation to occasional judgment.

Alignment is not harmony.
It is direction that remains visible when
  conditions tighten.

What follows is not about agreeing more.

It is about moving together without needing to be reminded why.

Sarah learned that when priorities stayed unspoken at work, they resurfaced at home as impatience she couldn't explain.

INTERLUDE: WHEN PRESSURE RETURNS
When Endurance Becomes Identity

There is a moment most leaders don't notice when it happens.

The work is finally steadier. Decisions hold longer. Fewer things escalate. The systems that once depended on constant intervention begin to function without visible strain. From the outside, it looks like progress.

Internally, something else can surface.

Leaders who have carried pressure for a long time often discover that endurance has become part of how they know themselves. Not as a burden, but as proof. They are the ones who stay late, step in early, and absorb disruption so others can keep moving. They are reliable because they are available. Necessary because they are willing.

When structure begins to hold, that identity is quietly challenged.

There is less urgency to respond to. Fewer moments that demand immediate correction. The work no longer requires constant compensation. What remains is space—space that can feel unfamiliar, even uncomfortable. Without the steady pull of pressure, leaders can feel momentarily unmoored.

This is rarely named as loss, but it can feel like one.

Endurance has a way of disguising itself as purpose. It gives leaders a clear role in moments of strain. It tells them where to stand when things tighten. When that role diminishes, the question becomes harder to answer: *What does leadership look like when it is no longer defined by carrying everything?*

Some leaders respond by filling the space. They reinsert themselves. They translate when translation is no longer required. They take on work that could now hold elsewhere. Not because the structure has failed, but because the old identity still fits.

Others hesitate long enough to notice what the space makes possible.

Without constant strain, attention widens. Judgment slows. Leaders can observe the system rather than stabilize it. They can see patterns that were invisible while endurance was the primary demand. This is where leadership shifts again—not toward effort, but toward trust.

This moment is not a turning point in the dramatic sense. Nothing breaks if it is missed. The work will continue either way. But how leaders respond here determines whether structure becomes durable or merely temporary.

Endurance is useful.

It is not meant to be permanent.

What follows is not about eliminating pressure.
It is about learning who you are when pressure is no longer the thing that proves your value.

CHAPTER 7

When Pressure Returns

When Pressure Returns

Pressure never resolves permanently. It recedes, reorganizes, and returns—often through a different door.

Leaders sometimes mistake periods of steadiness for completion. Systems feel clearer. Decisions hold. The work moves with less friction. Then conditions shift. Volume increases. Constraints tighten. An unexpected demand interrupts the rhythm that had begun to feel reliable.

This return of pressure is not a failure of containment, capacity, or alignment. It is a test of whether those disciplines were embedded deeply enough to adapt without reverting to heroics. When pressure resurfaces, it reveals what was learned—and what was merely resting.

The first signs are subtle. Old habits resurface under stress. Leaders step in earlier than necessary. Translation creeps back into conversations. Endurance is quietly reactivated as a safety mechanism.

The question is not whether pressure returns.
It always does.

The question is whether leadership responds by carrying more—or by letting the structure do the work it was built to hold.

When Old Patterns Reassert Themselves

The return of pressure is rarely dramatic. It doesn't arrive as collapse. It arrives as familiarity.

José noticed it in how quickly he stepped back into old roles. A deadline tightened, a dependency slipped, and he was suddenly the one reconnecting threads the system had been designed to hold. Not because the structure had failed, but because the habit was still available.

Nothing broke. The work continued. That was the danger.

What resurfaced wasn't chaos, but competence under strain—the reflex to absorb, translate, and compensate. The system accepted the help without resistance. It always does. Patterns don't disappear simply because better ones exist.

What mattered was not that the pattern returned, but how quickly it was recognized. José paused before fully stepping back in. He asked what the structure was meant to carry, and whether this moment truly required personal intervention.

Pressure receded again, not through effort, but through restraint. The structure held—not because it was perfect, but because it was trusted long enough to adjust.

Regression, he realized, is not the opposite of progress. It is the place where progress is tested.

When Trust Is Tested, Not Intentions

The real test did not arrive as a crisis. It arrived as a choice.

A new constraint surfaced—external, unavoidable, and poorly timed. The structure that had been built could absorb it, but only if leaders resisted the urge to intervene early. The temptation was familiar: step in, smooth the edges, keep momentum intact.

What made this moment different was not confidence in the plan, but restraint in response. Leaders watched how the system reacted before correcting it. Gaps surfaced. Some decisions slowed. A few assumptions were challenged in real time.

Nothing collapsed.

What emerged instead was unevenness—the kind that precedes learning. Teams adjusted locally. Tradeoffs were surfaced rather than escalated. The structure flexed without being bypassed.

Trust, it turned out, was not about believing people would do the right thing. It was about allowing the work to reveal where clarity was still insufficient. Intervention would have preserved short-term stability. Waiting preserved long-term capacity.

Pressure receded again, not because it was resolved, but because it was carried where it belonged.

A COMPOSITE CASE:
When Pressure Returns Differently

In a national nonprofit, a period of stability followed a major reorganization. Roles were clearer. Decision rights were documented. Teams operated with less friction than they had in years.

The return of pressure did not look like the past. Funding timelines tightened. External partners introduced new reporting requirements. None of it resembled the crisis that had prompted the earlier restructuring. That difference made the pressure harder to recognize.

Leaders responded cautiously at first. The structure still held, but only unevenly. Some teams adapted quickly. Others escalated decisions that previously would have been resolved locally. Old habits surfaced quietly, not as breakdowns, but as preferences for speed over clarity.

What mattered was not eliminating these regressions, but noticing them without panic. Leaders resisted the urge to correct immediately. Instead, they observed where the structure bent and where it quietly disappeared. Small adjustments followed—clarifying one decision boundary, revisiting one tradeoff that no longer fit current constraints.

The organization did not return to crisis. It also did not return to its earlier version of stability. It entered a different rhythm—one where pressure was expected to change form, and leadership responded by tuning the structure rather than replacing it.

Durability did not mean holding the line.
It meant learning where the line needed to move.

REFLECTION

1. When pressure returns, what old habits are most tempting for you to re-adopt?

2. Where do you intervene quickly—not because the structure failed, but because waiting feels unfamiliar?

3. What signals help you distinguish between a system that needs support and one that needs restraint?

PRACTICE

1. The next time pressure shifts, pause before intervening and ask what the structure is meant to absorb in this moment. Name what would be learned by waiting.

2. Identify one recent instance where endurance replaced trust. Consider what would need to be clarified so restraint becomes possible next time.

When Restraint Holds

Pressure does not undo the work that came before it. It reveals whether that work was built to endure.

When pressure returns, leaders are tempted to reclaim familiar roles—to absorb, translate, and steady what already feels unstable. Those responses are understandable. They are also costly when repeated without reflection. Endurance can restore motion quickly, but it rarely restores proportion.

What sustains leadership over time is not the absence of regression, but the ability to recognize it without panic. Structure does not fail because it bends. It fails when leaders bypass it out of habit rather than necessity.

Durability shows itself in restraint. In waiting long enough to see what the system can hold. In trusting clarity even when speed would feel reassuring. This is where leadership becomes less visible, but more effective.

Pressure will return again.

What changes is not the demand—but how much of it leadership is required to carry personally.

INTERLUDE:
What Comes Home

Miguel learned to recognize pressure before he learned to name it.

He noticed it in tone first. Conversations that shortened. Evenings that filled with silence instead of stories. Adults who were present but elsewhere, eyes still tracking decisions that had already ended.

Sarah felt it most clearly at the door. The workday didn't stop when she arrived home; it softened just enough to pass through. Coordination followed her—who needed what, what hadn't been resolved, what would require another explanation later. Her children learned to wait for her attention not because she asked them to, but because it arrived delayed. The boundary between work and home didn't disappear. It thinned.

Her former partner noticed it differently. Not in missed logistics, but in how quickly she tired of clarifying herself. Alignment failures at work reappeared as impatience at home—not because she cared less, but because she had already spent the day translating priorities that should have been clear.

José experienced the shift in speed. Decisions came quickly now. Too quickly. There was relief in that efficiency, and also distance. Evenings became quieter, shorter. Conversations moved past each other instead of toward understanding. Endurance had taught him how to keep things moving. It had not taught him how to stay.

None of this showed up as crisis. No one would have called it failure. These were small erosions—subtle enough to be normalized, familiar enough to be ignored.

Pressure rarely announces where it is going next. When it is not held at work, it migrates. It shows up in tone, in absence, in the narrowing of patience. Children learn to read it. Partners adjust around it. Homes reorganize themselves quietly in response.

Leadership that relies on endurance often protects outcomes while exposing relationships. Leadership that builds structure does something quieter. It protects presence.

This is not about balance or boundaries. It is about where strain is allowed to live. When work can hold what it creates, leaders return home with something left. Not answers. Not energy.

Attention.

CHAPTER 8

Trustwork

When Leadership Becomes Seasonal

Most leadership models assume continuity. They describe progress as linear and improvement as cumulative. Under sustained pressure, neither assumption holds.

Leadership moves in seasons. There are periods of building, periods of holding, periods of repair, and periods of restraint. Each season asks for a different posture. What creates strain is not the season itself, but the expectation that one posture should suffice for all of them.

When leaders mistake endurance for permanence, they overextend in seasons that require patience. When they mistake clarity for completion, they stop tending to the structures that made clarity possible in the first place. Pressure exposes these mismatches quickly.

Seasonal leadership does not mean inconsistency. It means discernment. Leaders learn to recognize when to intervene, when to wait, and when to let structure do the work it was designed to carry. This recognition is not intuitive. It is learned through attention to pattern rather than outcome.

This chapter is not about anticipating every change. It is about noticing when the posture that once worked is no longer the one the moment requires.

Durability depends less on strength than on timing.

When Trust Is Built Quietly

Trust is often associated with intention—belief in people, confidence in character, optimism about outcomes. In practice, trustwork is less about what leaders believe and more about what they allow the system to hold without supervision.

Trust builds quietly when leaders resist correcting work that is still forming. When they allow decisions to travel farther before being reviewed. When they accept short-term unevenness in exchange for long-term reliability. These choices rarely register as trust in the moment. They feel like restraint.

What makes this difficult is that trustwork rarely produces immediate affirmation. Progress can slow. Outcomes vary. The absence of intervention can feel indistinguishable from disengagement, especially in cultures accustomed to constant responsiveness.

Over time, the effects become visible in different ways. Teams begin to anticipate tradeoffs rather than escalate them. Decisions arrive better formed. Leaders are pulled in less frequently, but more deliberately. The work holds longer because it has learned how.

Trust, in this sense, is not relational warmth.
It is structural confidence.

And like all confidence built through experience, it grows only when leaders are willing to risk not being needed in every moment.

When Trust Is Withheld Carefully

José learned that trust is not extended all at once. It is calibrated.

Earlier in his leadership, trust had meant delegation—handing off responsibility and expecting follow-through. Under pressure, that approach often failed quietly. Work returned incomplete, escalations resurfaced, and trust narrowed instead of deepening.

What changed was not his belief in people, but his attention to readiness. Trust became conditional without becoming punitive. Decisions were shared alongside the reasoning behind them. Boundaries were clarified before authority was transferred. Support was available, but not automatic.

This approach felt slower at first. It required more observation and fewer assumptions. José resisted stepping in when outcomes were still forming, even when doing so would have produced faster resolution. Over time, the pattern shifted.

Fewer decisions returned half-shaped. When escalation occurred, it arrived with context.

Trust, he realized, grows when leaders are willing to be precise about what they are entrusting—and when. Withholding trust indiscriminately creates fear. Extending it indiscriminately creates fragility. The work of trust sits between those extremes.

Trustwork is not generosity.

It is judgment exercised over time.

What Trustwork Is Not

Trustwork is often misunderstood because its effects are indirect.

It is not delegation alone. Assigning responsibility without ensuring clarity simply relocates risk. When authority is handed off without shared criteria, trust is replaced by exposure. Outcomes may still arrive, but reliability does not.

It is not permissiveness. Allowing everything to proceed unchecked creates ambiguity rather than confidence. Teams may feel free, but freedom without boundaries leaves people guessing where judgment actually lives.

Trustwork is not optimism. Believing things will work out does not make them more likely to do so. Trust that depends on hope collapses under pressure. Trust that depends on structure adapts.

It is also not disengagement. Stepping back without remaining attentive can feel indistinguishable from absence.

Trustwork requires leaders to stay oriented—to notice patterns, not to manage outcomes.

Trustwork is disciplined. It involves deciding when to intervene, when to wait, and when to adjust the conditions under which decisions are made. When trust is treated as a posture rather than a practice, it becomes fragile.

A COMPOSITE CASE:
Trust That Holds Over Time

In a growing technology services firm, leaders had invested heavily in alignment. Decision rights were clearer. Escalation paths were documented. For a time, the system held.

As the organization expanded, trust began to thin—not because of failure, but because of pace. New managers inherited authority faster than judgment could be observed. Leaders responded by checking in more frequently, reviewing work earlier, and narrowing decision latitude to prevent mistakes.

The effect was subtle. Teams complied. Outcomes arrived. But learning slowed. Decisions returned upward half-formed, shaped to anticipate approval rather than exercise judgment. Trust had become conditional on reassurance.

The shift came when leaders resisted correcting too early. They clarified criteria instead of outcomes. They allowed some unevenness to persist long enough to see where readiness was real and where support was still required. Not every decision improved immediately. Over time, fewer decisions needed review at all.

Trust did not increase because leaders believed more. It increased because leaders waited longer to intervene.

The system became quieter. Leaders were less visible day to day, but more influential where judgment mattered most. Trustwork, sustained this way, did not accelerate growth. It stabilized it.

REFLECTION

1. Where in your work do you intervene early—not because outcomes are at risk, but because waiting feels uncomfortable?

2. What decisions currently return to you half-formed, and what might that suggest about how trust is being calibrated?

3. Where could clarity of criteria replace review of outcomes without increasing risk?

PRACTICE

1. Identify one recurring decision you review early. Clarify the criteria for success, then delay intervention long enough to observe judgment forming.
2. For one week, notice where reassurance substitutes for trust. Ask what would need to change structurally for reassurance to become unnecessary.

When Trust Holds

Trust is not established by intent or reinforced through reassurance. It is built through repeated moments where leaders choose restraint over correction and clarity over control.

When trustwork is practiced over time, leadership becomes less visible but more consequential. Decisions travel farther before returning. Judgment forms closer to the work. Leaders are engaged not because everything requires review, but because what reaches them matters.

This kind of trust does not remove risk. It redistributes it. Learning happens earlier. Errors surface sooner.

Responsibility becomes shared rather than absorbed. What holds is not confidence in people alone, but confidence in the conditions under which decisions are made.

> Trustwork does not ask leaders to disappear.
> It asks them to remain present without
> being central.

Over time, that posture changes not only how work moves, but how leadership is experienced—by teams, by organizations, and by those who live alongside the work long after decisions are made.

CHAPTER 9

When Leadership Is No Longer Central

When Leadership Is No Longer Central.

As systems mature, leadership changes position.

Earlier chapters described how containment, capacity, alignment, and trust redistribute pressure. Over time, those disciplines begin to do something quieter. They reduce how often leadership needs to be present at the center of work. Decisions hold longer. Direction remains visible. Fewer moments require immediate intervention.

This shift can feel disorienting. Leaders accustomed to being essential may interpret decreased visibility as loss of influence. In reality, it is evidence of integration. The work no longer depends on constant leadership input to remain coherent.

What replaces centrality is stewardship. Leaders pay attention to patterns rather than incidents. They intervene less frequently, but with greater consequence. Their role becomes one of tending—adjusting structure, revisiting tradeoffs, and noticing where conditions have changed enough to warrant recalibration.

Leadership at this stage is less reactive and more temporal. It considers not only what is needed now, but what will still hold later. Authority is expressed through restraint and timing rather than presence.

This chapter begins where many leadership models end: not with visibility, but with continuity

When Time Becomes the Constraint

Early leadership decisions are often evaluated by immediacy. Did the problem resolve? Did the team respond? Did work continue moving? As leadership matures, those measures become insufficient.

Time introduces a different constraint. Decisions made quickly can solve today's issue while creating tomorrow's instability. Structures that work under current conditions may erode quietly as volume, complexity, or expectations shift. What once held begins to thin—not through failure, but through accumulation.

Leaders who remain central tend to optimize for the present. Leaders who steward systems begin to notice duration. They ask how long a pattern has been required to hold, not just whether it works now. They attend to fatigue, repetition, and drift as indicators that conditions have changed.

This orientation alters how leadership attention is used. Fewer decisions are made in response to urgency alone. More are made with an eye toward what will still function when leadership is less available. Time becomes part of the decision, not a backdrop to it.

Durable leadership is not defined by speed.
It is defined by what remains coherent
after attention moves elsewhere.

When Leaders Step Back on Purpose

Sarah noticed the change not in outcomes, but in rhythm.

There were fewer urgent requests. Fewer moments that required immediate interpretation. Decisions reached her later, and with more shape. At first, this felt like distance. She worried she might be losing touch with the work.

What she was actually seeing was maturation.

Teams had begun to hold uncertainty longer. They surfaced tradeoffs without prompting. When they escalated, they did so with clarity about what they had already considered. Sarah's involvement shifted from resolving to confirming—from managing motion to stewarding direction.

Stepping back required discipline. The impulse to reinsert herself never disappeared. It softened as trust in the system deepened. Each time she resisted intervening too early, the work adjusted a little more on its own.

This did not make leadership passive. It made it temporal. Sarah's attention moved toward patterns—where decisions stalled repeatedly, where clarity thinned over time, where conditions had changed enough to require structural adjustment.

> Leadership, she realized, does not become
>   less demanding as systems mature.
> It becomes more deliberate.

What Stewardship Is Not

Stewardship is often mistaken for detachment.

When leaders step back, it can appear as disengagement to those accustomed to constant presence. In reality, stewardship requires more attention, not less—attention directed toward conditions rather than events.

Stewardship is not abdication. Decisions do not disappear simply because leaders intervene less frequently. Authority remains active, expressed through the design and maintenance of structures that guide action when leadership is not immediately available.

It is also not neutrality. Stewards do not avoid tension or defer difficult tradeoffs. They make those tradeoffs explicit early, so the work does not resolve them implicitly later through strain or conflict.

Stewardship is not patience alone. Waiting without observation is passivity. Stewardship requires noticing when patterns repeat, when friction accumulates, and when conditions have shifted enough to require recalibration.

When stewardship is misunderstood as distance, leaders are pulled back toward centrality. When it is understood as responsibility extended over time, leadership gains reach without regaining weight.

Stewardship Over Time

In a national professional services firm, leadership succession had been managed carefully. Decision rights were clear. Escalation thresholds were documented. For several years, the system functioned with little disruption.

As senior leaders transitioned out of day-to-day involvement, pressure did not spike. Instead, it diffused. Middle leaders absorbed more responsibility. Decisions took slightly longer, but arrived with more context. What changed most was not pace, but expectation.

New tensions surfaced around ownership. When outcomes faltered, it was no longer obvious who would step in to resolve them. Leaders resisted the impulse to reclaim centrality. Instead, they observed where uncertainty lingered and where authority needed clearer definition.

Small adjustments followed. One approval boundary was revised. One recurring decision was reclassified as local rather than senior. These changes were unremarkable in isolation. Over time, they compounded.

The firm did not become faster.
It became more coherent.

Stewardship showed itself not through decisive moments, but through sustained attention to what the system needed to carry next—without assuming leadership would always be there to compensate.

REFLECTION

---

1. Where in your work do you remain central out of habit rather than necessity?

2. Which decisions still require your presence because the conditions for stewardship are not yet in place?

3. Where has time—not urgency—become the most important constraint you are managing?

PRACTICE

1. Identify one decision you currently hold that could travel farther without loss of quality. Clarify what would need to be visible for you to step back with confidence.

2. Over the next two weeks, notice patterns rather than incidents. Track what repeats, not what interrupts.

When Stewardship Holds

Leadership does not mature by accumulating more responsibility. It matures by learning where responsibility can live without constant supervision.

As systems stabilize, the temptation is to remain central—to preserve coherence by staying close to every decision. Stewardship asks for a different posture. One that trusts what has been built long enough to see how it holds across time, not just under immediate pressure.

This work is rarely visible. It unfolds in rhythm rather than event, in patterns rather than moments. Leaders pay attention to what repeats, what thins, and what no longer fits the conditions it once served. They intervene less often, but with greater consequence.

Stewardship is not withdrawal.
It is leadership extended forward—designed
to hold when attention moves elsewhere.

CHAPTER 10

When Leadership Is Designed to Outlast You

When Leadership Is Designed to Outlast You

Most leadership conversations end at succession. Roles transfer. Authority moves. The organization continues. What is rarely examined is whether the way leadership has been practiced can endure once the leader is no longer present to correct, interpret, or stabilize it.

Leadership that outlasts an individual is not sustained by values statements or continuity plans. It is sustained by conditions that allow judgment to travel without distortion. When structure, clarity, and trust are embedded deeply enough, leadership does not disappear with the leader. It redistributes.

This requires a different orientation to influence. Leaders stop optimizing for personal effectiveness and begin designing for absence. They ask what will still hold when they are not in the room, not on the call, not available to decide. That question shifts attention from performance to inheritance.

Designing leadership to outlast you does not diminish responsibility. It reframes it. Decisions are shaped with longer consequences in mind. Tradeoffs are made explicit so they do not rely on memory. The work becomes legible enough to guide action without constant reinforcement.

This chapter moves beyond stewardship of the present.

It asks what kind of leadership remains when presence is no longer the primary stabilizer.

When Leadership Is Meant to Be Inherited

Legacy is often framed as what leaders leave behind. In practice, it is what others are able to carry forward without explanation.

Inherited leadership does not rely on memory or personality. It depends on whether the work has been shaped clearly enough that judgment can be exercised without reenacting past decisions. When tradeoffs are explicit, priorities remain visible even as people change.

This shifts how leaders use authority. Instead of solving problems decisively, they focus on making decisions legible. They name why a boundary exists, not just where it sits. They clarify which tensions are structural and which are situational, so successors are not forced to rediscover them through failure.

Inheritance also requires restraint. Not every insight needs to be codified. Some understanding must remain experiential. Leaders decide carefully what must be preserved precisely and what must be allowed to adapt. Too much prescription creates fragility. Too little clarity creates drift.

> Leadership meant to be inherited is not
> about permanence.
> It is about continuity that can survive
> reinterpretation.

When Leadership Touches Life Beyond Work

Miguel noticed the difference before he could name it.

Evenings were quieter. Not easier—just steadier. His father still carried responsibility, but it no longer followed him home with the same intensity. Decisions stayed at work. Attention returned in small, ordinary ways that had once been crowded out by urgency.

Nothing dramatic had changed. There was no declaration, no boundary announced. What shifted was how leadership had been structured during the day. Fewer late escalations. Fewer unresolved tensions carried forward. When leadership stopped absorbing what systems could hold, presence became available again.

The cost of leadership is often measured professionally—burnout, turnover, performance. Its effects are felt elsewhere first. In patience that shortens. In attention that thins. In relationships that absorb pressure without context.

Leadership designed to outlast you does more than preserve organizations. It protects the lives that surround the work. When judgment is exercised upstream, fewer decisions leak downstream into places they were never meant to live.

Legacy, in this sense, is not symbolic.
It is lived.

What Legacy Is Not

Legacy is often confused with permanence.

When leaders talk about legacy, they frequently describe what should remain unchanged—values, practices, or decisions preserved as proof of success. In reality, leadership that cannot be adapted rarely survives intact. What remains rigid becomes brittle.

Legacy is not control extended beyond tenure. Attempting to govern future decisions through excessive documentation or fixed rules places a burden on successors rather than supporting them. It signals mistrust of judgment rather than confidence in it.

It is also not self-sacrifice. Leadership that demands ongoing personal cost—long after conditions could have been redesigned—leaves an inheritance of depletion. Over time, that cost is absorbed by families, teams, and systems that were never meant to carry it.

A durable legacy does not require replication. It requires orientation.

When leaders focus on making tradeoffs visible and tensions explicit, they leave behind something more usable than instruction: a way of seeing the work clearly enough to decide again.

A COMPOSITE CASE:
What Remains After Leadership Moves On

In a regional healthcare organization, a long-tenured executive prepared to step out of daily leadership. The team had weathered years of complexity together—regulatory shifts, staffing shortages, rapid growth. The concern was not whether the next leader would be capable, but whether the work itself would remain coherent.

Rather than documenting every decision, the outgoing leader focused on surfacing tensions that had shaped past choices. Where speed had been traded for safety. Where autonomy had been limited to preserve coordination. These tradeoffs were named repeatedly, in meetings and handoffs, not as instructions but as orientation.

After the transition, the organization did not operate exactly the same. Some decisions were made differently. A few boundaries moved. What held was not uniformity, but judgment. Leaders recognized familiar tensions and navigated them without needing approval from the past.

Months later, the absence was noticeable—but not disruptive. Work continued with fewer escalations than expected. When challenges surfaced, they arrived with context. The system did not preserve the leader's decisions.

It preserved the leader's way of seeing.

REFLECTION

1. If you were to step away from your current role for six months, what aspects of your judgment would others struggle to recreate without you?

2. Which recurring decisions depend on your memory rather than shared orientation?

3. Where might clearer articulation of tradeoffs reduce the need for future correction or explanation?

PRACTICE

1. Identify one decision pattern that has shaped your leadership. Name the tension it resolves and document *why* it exists rather than *how* it should be handled.

2. Notice where personal endurance has substituted for structural clarity. Ask what would need to change for that endurance to become unnecessary.

When Leadership Outlasts You

Leadership that is designed to outlast an individual does not attempt to preserve decisions. It preserves orientation.

What remains is not a set of answers, but a way of seeing—an ability to recognize familiar tensions, weigh tradeoffs, and act without requiring the past to intervene. This kind of leadership does not constrain successors. It equips them.

The most durable legacy is not continuity of behavior, but continuity of judgment. When leaders invest in clarity that can be carried forward, they reduce the need for correction, explanation, and personal sacrifice. The work learns how to hold itself.

This is not a withdrawal from responsibility.

It is responsibility extended beyond presence.

Leadership shaped this way does more than endure change. It makes change navigable—for organizations, for relationships, and for the lives that continue alongside the work.

CHAPTER 11

Working Frame

When Leadership Protects What It Cannot Replace

There is a point where leadership stops being about optimization and becomes about protection.

Earlier chapters focused on designing work to hold—through structure, trust, stewardship, and inheritance. Over time, another responsibility becomes unavoidable. Leaders must decide what should no longer be consumed by the work, even if it could be.

Not all costs are visible on balance sheets or performance reviews. Some appear slowly, as diminished patience, shortened attention, or relationships that absorb pressure without consent. These costs are rarely intentional. They accumulate when leadership remains oriented toward output long after conditions have changed.

Protective leadership begins with recognition. Leaders notice when endurance has replaced judgment and when sacrifice has become normalized rather than necessary. They ask not only what the work requires, but what it should not be allowed to take.

This is not a retreat from ambition.
It is a redefinition of responsibility.

Leadership that protects what cannot be replaced—health, presence, trust—creates boundaries that allow the work to continue without quietly extracting more than it should.

When the Work Starts Taking More Than It Gives

The signal is rarely dramatic.

Work does not announce when it has crossed from demanding to consuming. It shows up indirectly—through shortened patience at home, through conversations postponed, through attention that never fully returns. Leaders often notice these changes last, because they have learned to absorb strain quietly.

What makes this difficult is that the work continues to reward endurance. Problems get solved. Progress is made. Responsibility is reinforced. From the outside, nothing appears wrong. From the inside, something begins to thin.

At this stage, leadership choices are no longer neutral. Allowing the work to continue extracting more time, focus, or emotional capacity is itself a decision. Not because leaders intend harm, but because unexamined endurance becomes permission.

Protective leadership names this moment without dramatizing it. It recognizes that some costs are irreversible once crossed. Relationships do not recover on the same timeline as projects. Health does not replenish on quarterly cycles. Presence, once eroded, is not easily restored.

The work will always ask for more.
Leadership decides when the answer
  must become no.

When Leadership Draws a Line

José did not notice the boundary forming all at once.

It emerged gradually, through small refusals that felt out of character at first. A meeting declined late in the evening. A deadline renegotiated rather than absorbed. An escalation returned with a request for clarification instead of immediate resolution.

None of these choices altered the trajectory of the work in obvious ways. What changed was where pressure was allowed to land. José stopped carrying decisions home that could wait until morning. He resisted translating organizational urgency into personal availability. Over time, the work adjusted.

The line was not drawn against responsibility.
It was drawn against quiet erosion.

Colleagues adapted. Some initially interpreted the shift as distance. What they encountered instead was consistency. Expectations became clearer. Tradeoffs were named earlier. When José was present, he was fully present. When he was not, the system held.

Protective leadership does not announce boundaries dramatically. It establishes them steadily, through repeated decisions that signal what will—and will not—be absorbed.

A line drawn this way is rarely defended.
It is respected.

What Protection Is Not

Protection is often misunderstood as withdrawal.

When leaders set limits, it can appear as disengagement to those accustomed to constant access. In reality, protection requires sustained attention—attention directed toward what must be preserved, not simply what must be delivered.

Protection is not avoidance. Leaders do not step away from difficult decisions; they refuse to resolve them by absorbing their cost personally. When pressure is consistently carried by individuals rather than structures, it is not leadership—it is substitution.

It is also not inflexibility. Protective boundaries are not rigid rules imposed once and defended indefinitely. They are living constraints, adjusted as conditions change. What remains constant is the commitment to prevent quiet erosion from becoming normalized.

Protection is not self-interest. The benefits extend outward. Teams gain clearer expectations. Relationships regain steadiness. Systems learn where responsibility belongs rather than where it can be pushed.

When protection is mistaken for distance, leaders are pulled back toward overextension. When it is understood as stewardship of what cannot be replaced, leadership becomes more sustainable—for the work and for the people who carry it.

A COMPOSITE CASE:
Choosing What the Work Cannot Take

In a fast-growing professional services organization, leadership had become synonymous with availability. Senior leaders were responsive at all hours. Decisions moved quickly. Clients felt supported. The system appeared strong.

Over time, the cost became harder to ignore. Leaders were present, but strained. Turnover increased quietly among mid-level managers. At home, patience shortened. At work, urgency filled gaps where clarity had thinned.

The turning point did not come from a crisis. It came from recognition. Leaders acknowledged that responsiveness had replaced structure, and that endurance had become the default solution to every constraint. The work was not failing. It was consuming.

Instead of asking leaders to give less, the organization redesigned how pressure was handled. Escalation paths were clarified. Late-stage decisions were reclassified. Availability expectations were narrowed deliberately. Some discomfort followed. Not everything moved as quickly.

What changed was where the cost landed. Pressure that had been absorbed personally was redistributed structurally. Leaders became less reactive and more precise. Over time, retention stabilized. Decision quality improved. At home, presence returned.

Protection did not weaken the work.
It made it livable.

REFLECTION

1. Where in your life has endurance quietly replaced judgment as the primary way work gets done?

2. What costs are being absorbed personally that could be redistributed structurally without reducing responsibility?

3. Which boundaries would feel uncomfortable to set—not because they are wrong, but because they would expose where pressure currently lives?

PRACTICE

1. Identify one recurring moment where work spills into personal time by default. Clarify what structural adjustment—not personal sacrifice—would prevent that spillover.

2. Over the next two weeks, notice where saying yes preserves momentum but erodes presence. Ask what condition would need to change for the yes to become unnecessary.

When Protection Holds

Leadership eventually confronts a limit it cannot negotiate away.

Not every demand should be met. Not every cost should be absorbed. When work begins to consume what cannot be replaced—health, presence, trust—leadership responsibility shifts. The question is no longer how much can be carried, but what must be protected for the work to remain viable.

Protective leadership does not retreat from responsibility. It clarifies it. Boundaries become expressions of judgment rather than refusals of effort. Pressure is redirected to where it can be held without quiet erosion.

What this kind of leadership safeguards is not comfort. It safeguards continuity.

When leaders protect what cannot be replaced, they make it possible for the work—and the lives around it—to continue without steadily diminishing what makes leadership worth sustaining

CHAPTER 12

Final Chapter

What Leadership Was Always For

By this point, leadership has been stripped of performance.

What remains is not technique or posture, but responsibility carried with discernment. Across containment, capacity, alignment, trust, stewardship, legacy, and protection, a single pattern has emerged: leadership exists to create conditions where work can proceed without quietly consuming what sustains it.

This reframes leadership's purpose.

Leadership is not primarily about influence, visibility, or endurance. It is about placement—deciding where pressure belongs, where judgment must live, and where limits protect continuity rather than impede progress. When these decisions are made well, leadership becomes less dramatic and more consequential.

The measure of leadership, then, is not how much it absorbs, but what it allows others to carry without distortion.

Systems mature. People regain presence. Work holds longer without demanding constant intervention.

This final chapter does not offer resolution.

It offers orientation—so leadership can be practiced with clarity about what it is meant to serve, and what it must never quietly take.

When Work and Life Stop Competing

The separation between leadership at work and presence at home is often treated as a personal skill. Leaders are encouraged to manage boundaries better, compartmentalize more effectively, or recover faster. These approaches assume the tension is internal.

More often, it is structural.

When pressure is carried in the right places during the day, it does not need to be processed later at night. When decisions are resolved where they arise, they do not follow leaders home in fragments. What appears as balance is frequently the byproduct of design.

This does not eliminate strain. It changes where strain lives. Leadership that places pressure deliberately allows attention to return when it is no longer required elsewhere. Presence becomes possible not because leaders try harder, but because fewer unresolved demands remain.

Over time, this integration alters how leadership is experienced across domains. Work no longer borrows against relationships. Home life no longer absorbs organizational ambiguity. Each regains its proper weight.

Integration, in this sense, is not harmony.
It is clarity about what belongs where.

What Remains When the Work Is Done Well

When leadership is practiced with restraint, something unexpected becomes visible.

The work does not disappear. Complexity remains. Decisions still carry consequence. What changes is the residue. Less urgency leaks into places it does not belong. Fewer conversations are deferred without explanation. Attention returns more fully because it is no longer fragmented by unresolved demands.

What remains is not ease, but steadiness. Leaders recognize familiar tensions without rushing to resolve them prematurely. Teams carry judgment closer to the work. Structures hold longer before needing repair. The system becomes quieter, not because less is happening, but because less is being absorbed unnecessarily.

This steadiness extends beyond outcomes. It shapes how leadership is felt by others—through consistency, availability that is deliberate rather than constant, and boundaries that protect continuity instead of eroding it.

When the work is done well, leadership leaves fewer traces.

Not because it mattered less,
but because it was placed where it could hold.

What Remains

Leadership rarely announces when it is being done well.

There is no clear moment of arrival, no lasting resolution. What appears instead is continuity. Work moves without constant correction. Decisions are carried with judgment rather than urgency. Pressure lands where it can be held without quietly extracting more than it should.

This kind of leadership is not impressive in the moment. It is recognizable over time. In systems that endure change without collapsing into reactivity. In relationships that remain intact rather than strained by invisible cost. In leaders who are present where they are needed—and absent where they are not.

Nothing in this book argues for less responsibility.
It argues for responsibility placed deliberately.

When leadership is practiced this way, it does not demand constant attention. It leaves behind conditions that continue to work, even when leadership steps out of view.

What remains is not control or certainty.
What remains is clarity that holds.

How This Book Is Used

This book is not designed to be consumed quickly or applied mechanically. It is meant to be returned to as a reference for Judgment Leadership, especially when pressure rises, when responsibility becomes concentrated, or when decision quality begins to narrow.

Some readers will move through it sequentially. Others will open to the chapter that matches the condition they are navigating: containment when escalation increases, capacity when judgment thins, alignment when coordination becomes costly. Both patterns of engagement have appeared. The structure of the book allows for non-linear engagement without losing coherence.

Leaders often use this book privately, as a way to regain orientation when endurance has replaced judgment. In those moments, the language is intended to slow the reader just enough to notice where pressure is being carried personally rather than structurally.

Teams and facilitators use the book differently. Chapters are read together, often alongside real work, not as curriculum but as shared reference. The reflection and practice sections are not exercises to be completed, but prompts that create space for conversation—particularly when clarity feels present but fragile—without directing outcomes.

This book does not offer tools, templates, or step-by-step instruction. Its value lies in helping readers recognize patterns early, before pressure hardens into habit. Used this way, it becomes a stabilizing reference—one that supports leadership without asking to be followed.

On Use in Facilitators Settings

This book is often used in rooms where pressure is already present.

Used well, it gives groups a shared language for protecting decision integrity under pressure without turning the work into performance.

Facilitators and leaders who bring this work into teams, organizations, or learning environments tend to use it as a shared reference rather than a curriculum. Chapters are read alongside real conditions, not as models to be implemented, but as language that helps people notice patterns earlier and speak about them more clearly.

The material is intentionally non-prescriptive. Its value lies less in agreement than in orientation—helping groups recognize where pressure belongs, where judgment is being carried, and where structure may need attention.

This book is not a program.
It does not require alignment to be useful.

Used well, it supports conversations that would otherwise remain implicit, especially where responsibility is high and clarity is fragile.

Afterword

Pressure does not disappear. It changes shape.

Most leaders learn to manage this by becoming stronger, faster, or more available. That approach can work—for a while. Over time, the cost becomes harder to name and easier to accept. What begins as commitment quietly turns into erosion.

This book has argued for a different posture. One that treats pressure as information, not a personal test. One that builds structures capable of holding strain so leadership is not defined by how much can be absorbed.

The work described here is not dramatic. It does not resolve tension permanently or eliminate regression. It does something quieter and more durable. It creates conditions where judgment has room, where direction holds, and where restraint becomes a sign of trust rather than absence.

Leadership shaped this way protects more than outcomes. It protects attention, presence, and the relationships that feel pressure long after decisions are made.

Nothing in these pages promises ease.

What they offer is orientation—so when pressure returns, leaders are less likely to mistake endurance for responsibility, and more likely to recognize where the work itself can carry what it creates.

That recognition changes everything that follows.

About the Author

Dr. Hugo Velazco is an executive advisor who studies how leaders maintain decision integrity when responsibility cannot be delegated and outcomes remain uncertain. An Army veteran and organizational researcher, he has worked alongside leaders in high-accountability environments where pressure is persistent and consequences are real. His work develops the concept of **Judgment Leadership**: the discipline of sustaining decision integrity under pressure through clarity, containment, and responsibility aligned with authority.

An ICF Professional Certified Coach (PCC) and Army veteran, Dr. Velazco brings experience from human resources, organizational leadership, and applied business psychology. He has worked across public, private, and non-profit systems where leadership decisions carry long-term organizational impact.

He is the founder of Coaching360x, an advisory practice focused on judgment, authority alignment, and leadership clarity under pressure. His work is known for its calm, direct posture and its resistance to oversimplified solutions.

Dr. Velazco lives and works in Southern California. More information can be found at

Coaching360x.com

After Orientation

This book is designed to stand on its own. It offers a language for **Judgment Leadership**, so leaders can recognize when pressure is distorting judgment and restore decision integrity before the cost becomes personal.

It does not require supplementary materials, exercises, or tools to be useful. Its value lies in how it shapes attention, judgment, and posture under pressure, rather than in what it instructs readers to do.

In some facilitated or organizational settings, a separate Facilitator's Companion may be used to support conversation alongside this book. That Companion is not a workbook, curriculum, or teaching guide, and it is not intended for general distribution. It exists solely to support facilitators in holding conversations with the same restraint and posture the book itself was written in.

Readers do not need access to any additional materials to engage fully with this book.

Acknowledgments

This book was shaped through conversations, observation, and time.

I am grateful to the leaders who trusted me with their thinking before trusting me with their words, and to the people who allowed their work to be examined with care.

Most of all, I thank my wife, **Lucero**, for her steadiness, patience, and clarity—especially in the moments when the work demanded more than it should have. And my son, **Abel**, whose presence has been a constant reminder of what leadership is ultimately meant to protect.

Thank you to those who understood restraint as care, and clarity as a form of respect.

ByThe Book Design | Designed by Anna Perotti
bythebookdesign.com

First edition

ISBN 979-8-9945441-0-5

To cite this work: Velazco, H. (2026). *Judgment Leadership: Decision Integrity Under Pressure.*

Published by Coaching360x LLC
Torrance, California